LORD, SAVE ME!

30 POEMS OF FAITH

Ray E. Groh

Lord, Save Me!
30 Poems of Faith

Ray E. Groh

(ISBN-13): 978-0-9903703-5-2

(softcover: 50# acid-free alkaline paper)

Cover design by Gwyn Snider ©

Interior design by Jean Groh ©

Edited by Jean Groh and Ray E. Groh

Manufactured in the United States of America.

Win By KO Publications

Iowa City, Iowa

winbykopublications.com

To the Lord, who stretches
out his hand when we cry out,
"Lord, save me!"

TABLE OF CONTENTS

INTRODUCTION

Jesus came toward them walking on the sea. When the disciples saw him, Peter said, "Lord, command me to come to you on the water." Jesus said, "Come." Peter got out of the boat and began to walk on the water toward him. But when he saw how strong the wind was he became frightened; and, beginning to sink, he cried out, "Lord, save me!" Immediately Jesus stretched out his hand and caught him, and said, "O you of little faith, why did you doubt?" - Mathew 14:22-33

Let us look at how this biblical passage applies to us. It said, Jesus came toward them. Jesus also comes to us; seeking us out, and what was Peter's response? He showed an eagerness to meet the Lord. We should imitate the example of Peter and have that same desire to meet the Lord in our hearts. But shortly after Peter approached Christ, what happened? He took his eyes off him. It is then that he starts to sink. Sink amidst the storm that surrounded him. Surely he would have died had Jesus not caught him. If we take our eyes off Christ we will also sink amidst the storms that surround us. The storm never disappeared for Peter, and it won't disappear for us either. We will always be in life's storm, even with Christ nearby, as in the case of Peter. But with Christ, we will always be safe and never sink.

In the above passage, after Peter calls For Jesus' help, it doesn't say that Jesus stretched out his hand and caught him. It says he, "**Immediately**, stretched out his hand and caught him." Jesus acted without hesitation, and he will do the same for us when we call on him in our time of need. Finally, Christ said, "O you of little faith, why did you doubt?" Let us take a lesson from this too. When we are in the midst of the storms in our life, let us also have faith and not doubt in the Lord. Trust in him that when we seek him out, we will be taken care of and triumph over the storms that threaten to harm us. No matter what the storms are, we shall not sink, if we too exclaim, "Lord, save me!"

May the poems in this book help the reader to know that no matter what they are going through, they are never alone. May they remind the reader to always look for Christ during the storm, and know that through this search is born the spark of hope. A spark that if fanned to a flame, will burn down the walls of pain and suffering. Remember, the brightest light always shines at the end of the darkest tunnel.

It is my intention that in times of trouble, when you are down, and life is at its darkest moment, you will not give up, but like Peter, seek the Lord, who is the solution to all our woes. For once we have found him, we will have hope!

HELP ME

Amidst the waters of the sea,

struggles a survivor like me.

The waves pound and beat me down,

and I sink and start to drown.

No passersby stop to help,

all ignore my splashing, struggles, and deathly yelp.

They have been placed on safe debris,

placed there, by the hands of me.

And yet they turn their backs in the sea,

turn them from myself, and to salvation they flee.

Only one outstretched hand reaches amidst the lot,

while others choose to help me not.

I reached and touched the outstretched fingers,

and know that with them, my life still lingers.

And from their compassion my life will not end,

because in this storm, I have a friend.

NOT ALONE

They have harassed you and called you every name,

singled you out, and gave you the blame.

Laughter, persecution, they have mocked,

friendship, compassion, mercy, they have blocked.

Upon you they have reined fists, kicks, and blows of hate,

left you helpless, beaten, and desolate.

You looked in the crowd for a friendly face,

but there was none to be found in that place.

Amidst this trial do not despair,

for I see thy life, and assure you, I am there.

Look not to these and waste your bother,

but tilt thy head upward, toward your heavenly father.

Cast your eyes to the cross at the right,

and you will see my guiding light.

Upon your cross raised on high,

look to me for an encouraging sigh.

When you see me beaten and hanging on mine of wood,

nailed, scourged, crowned with thorns, you'll have understood.

For I have said, take up thy cross and follow me,

leaving you these words, so you will truly see.

You will never be alone in times of strife,

if you embrace the Lord and his life.

For my wounds are the salve of all who suffer,

healing their ills with a spiritual buffer.

Raised on a cross by my enemies to die,

is my plan for you, to persevere through your trials, and continue to try.

THE JOURNEY

On the day of your birth,

you were baptized not for this earth.

Through the years as you grew,

it was your soul that I did pursue.

Clothed in flesh not your own,

for I gave it to you only on loan.

Inspiring you for much greater things,

to eventually fly on angel's wings.

And when a temptation did arise,

it was I who had advised you otherwise.

You resisted them and followed my way,

listening to your heart, and what it had to say.

Thus I guided you through this worldly land,

pointing out your path with my wounded hand.

And when at times you did fall,

it was my voice who gave the call.

On the ground where you did lay,

it was I who picked you up, for yet another day.

And I will continue to guide you as you roam,

till you are safe with me, in your heavenly home.

MY DISCIPLE

Your last coin you gave to another,

calling this stranger, the least of your brother.

When you were struck, they called you weak,

but I saw thy strength, as you gave the other cheek.

They laughed at you when you chose my way,

but I merely smiled, and marked the day.

You came to the aid of one who was in need,

while many passed by and took no heed.

When you heard lies, insults, and jokes of lewd,

you spoke of me to change the mood.

You wiped away every fallen tear,

with consoling words and heavenly cheer.

Lust, violence, greed, the world says more of the same,

but with each spouting, you always preached my name.

Continue on this bumpy road,

and your future will be foretold.

When you see the finish near,

place thy zeal into high gear.

Do not slow, do not stop, but continue to run,

until we meet at the finish, and I say, faithful servant, well done.

(The following poem was inspired when someone I knew was raped.)

THE JUST JUDGE

You suffered by those of hate,

but I assure you, they have sealed their fate.

They sprang from the darkness assured there was no light,

not realizing that all is within my sight.

From the first, their crimes had grown,

though concealing the act, their evil was made known.

You were alone when they made their attack,

but it is I, the just judge, who has got your back.

So think not that they have gotten away,

for I the Lord, will have the final say.

No detail escapes my sight,

not even those done, in the darkest of night.

As they stalked, hid, and went after you,

so to them I will follow, wait, and pursue.

Fear not after their deed they flew,

for I will strike when their time is due.

They will run and try to hide,

only to find me waiting at their side.

Their bodies will shake as their hearts race with fear,

sweat dripping from their brow, knowing my judgement is near.

Their sins will soon be read by me,

and try as they might, they will be unable to flee.

For their actions I will repay,

many times over what they did that day.

And should they show no repentance,

then I will pronounce their final sentence.

THE DISGUISES OF SATAN

My child you know of the devil and hell,

but I have something of importance that I need to tell.

Satan does not always come dressed to abhor,

sometimes he is clothed sweet and gentle, to present another door.

More fall from the honey he offers,

and are soon buried past the earth in his hellish coffers.

He gives money piled on high,

but the price tag is that that one must die.

Others he gives an abundance of sex,

but dear child, this is just a hex.

Many are given a rank of power,

but soon after, their life will go sour.

Drugs, depression, alcohol, sex,

are the prescription he writes on his checks.

Once they are cashed in his bank,

to many levels below his customers sank.

He offers jewels to entice,

and displays the flesh dressed to spice.

Turns over power to command,

and finally for that soul, he will demand.

Do not choose drugs, violence, and evils as your road,

nor the sweets of power, money, and sex, as I have told.

For Satan presents his path in different ways,
but beyond the final door is an eternal blaze.
My dear child follow my cross,
and in the end you will suffer no loss.
Though at times you may struggle and fall,
you will find your way back, hearing my call.
Keep steadfast upon my path,
and you will be free of Satan's wrath.
And when your world is finally done,
you will have eternal happiness, with me and my son.

THE GOOD SHEPHERD

My sheep have wandered far from my side,

out of my sight, their protection denied.

Into the unknown they will travel,

their peace soon to unravel.

The devil promises green pastures to lure them away,

enticing my sheep to wander and stray.

They know not what dangers lie ahead,

dangers that will leave them wounded, or even worse; dead.

It is the devil that attacks the fold not as a wolf or a bear,

but as one of their own, to ensure a snare.

But I will search my sheep and call them by name,

to rescue them from the enemy, I'll even die a death of shame.

Many miles and years I will comb,

to bring them back on my shoulders, safely home.

THE PASSION

Arrested in the garden when I was deep in prayer,

betrayed by one of my own, who told the enemy I was there.

He threw away my promise of eternal bliss,

in exchange for thirty coins of silver, with a betraying kiss.

Another follower denied knowing me three times,

leaving me alone to fend for myself, against trumped up crimes.

The rest that were once always at my side,

quickly scattered, to find a place to hide.

They took me away to file charges against me,

but the false witnesses that testified, could not agree.

Though they found no evidence no matter how hard they did try,

they never the less ordered me as deserving to die.

Placed before a judge who could find no wrong,

he decided to have me flogged, to satisfy a bloodthirsty throng.

They scourged me till my flesh was ripped apart,

slowly taking my life, but never my heart.

Then they crowned me with thorns that pierced deep into my head,

if not for my destiny, I would have been dead.

They spat on my face and struck my head with a reed,

mocked, punched, and plucked my beard, to fill their evil need.

Returned to the judge who put my fate into the hands of a heartless clan,

trying to solicit them to compassion, he showed them my beaten features, saying, "Behold the man!"

But the verdict was already in;

they had found me guilty before the trial was to begin.

But the only guilt I bear they know not of,

and that is my great undying love.

THE PASSION PART 2

I have been handed over and sentenced to die,

so much did they detest me that, "Crucify him," was their cry.

I gazed into the crowd with loving eyes,

but the stares they returned to me were, to you we despise.

Given a beam of heavy wood to bear,

was what my people gave me, to show how much they care.

Drained of my strength I fell under its weight,

landing on the rocks, didn't hurt as much as the hate.

They whipped and kicked me to arise,

until I got up, while hearing their lies.

Exhausted and trying to catch my breath,

I continued on, marching to my death.

They told me the goal in the distance was the cross,

but my goal was to save my people, and spare their souls the loss.

Roughly they stripped off my clothes,

tearing old wounds from past delivered blows.

They placed spikes on my limbs and pounded them in;

the force of the hammers was not from muscle, but from sin.

Impaled on the wood and raised on high,

mocked and insulted, from those who stood by.

As my blood fell to the ground and my life was slipping away,

I rejoiced in knowing that salvation came on this day.

THE HEAVENLY KEY

Lord, I am bound by the chains of sin,

and here I remain a prisoner, for a temptation I gave in.

The devil stands nearby smiling with glee,

for unto myself, I can never be free.

Lord, please help me,

for you alone hold the key.

My child long before you prayed,

I was coming to your aid.

Before my children even call,

I am on my way to prevent their fall.

I whisper in their ear with a guiding voice,

but yield to what is their choice.

And should they turn away from me,

I don't leave, but start to plea.

I encourage them to rethink their decision,

or suffer at the hands of the devil's derision.

Then with sorrowful eyes they return to me,

displaying their chains, asking to be set free.

They tell me there is no way to open the lock,

but I respond, there is nothing I won't do for my flock.

With no combination the devil laughs and shakes his head, nope, but I am the Christ, so with me, always have hope.

I have made the deaf hear, and gave sight to the blind,

the lame walk, and for other ills I have responded in kind.

But greater than these,

is what I do for those who fall on their knees.

I break the clasp,

of the chains that are in the devil's grasp.

Satan has different locks; lust, anger, greed, and more,

but I have one key that will open every door.

I place my wrist on the lock made of wood,

and it begins to give from the power of the eternal good.

My wrist opens and starts to bleed,

this is what is required for the soul in need.

There it remains bound on this cross,

so my dear child, thy shackles you can now toss.

(Inspired by someone I knew who as a child was molested. Later, they fell into a life of promiscuity that destroyed their marriage. Thankfully they found God)

THE PRODIGAL CHILD

In this life wanders a child,

meek, humble, and tenderly mild.

Innocent as the heavenly light,

when evil attacks, and casts its first deadly bite.

Injured, pained, and helpless to linger,

evil sees its prey, and strikes a second stinger.

Many are the passersby,

but no one notices, or stops for this child's cry.

Helpless, hurt, and tossed every which way,

the child falls, and begins to stray.

Older and older the child grows,

taking life's hard knocks, and more damaging blows.

But all has not been in vain,

for Christ takes a cross, and creates spiritual gain.

He rescues this soul as the Samaritan of yore,

and rests them in the wounds that he bore.

Safe in the holes of his flesh,

the soul heals and starts to refresh.

Pain, sadness, and being lost,

are reversed by the most priceless cost.

Blessings, miracles, peace, are the reward,

for the soul that rests in the Lord.

Thus he raises this soul from the dead,

giving new life, while his own body bled.

Then gently he returns the soul back on its way,

with a glow that shines brighter than before that sad day.

KNOCK AND YOU SHALL RECEIVE

Lord, why do things happen to me?

Dear child, I grant them so that you can see.

Lord, my sufferings are like a consuming flame.

Dear little one, I know well thy name.

Then why don't you hear my continued cries?

Oh, little one, I am aware of each and every one of your sighs.

I pray and plead,

I know you do, and will grant you what you need.

Now listen to my story,

as I tell it from my throne of glory.

You pray and I hear,

for it is I who hold you so very dear.

At the moment you may not see my aid,

but I see your prayers and petitions at my throne, where they've been laid.

I send my blessings and grace,

to restore your wounds, and comfort thy face.

The world is sinful and evil abounds,

hurting my little ones like blood thirsty hounds.

Evil has done the same to me,

just look at the crucifix, and tell me what you see.

I was scourged, crowned, and killed on a cross,

all of this, for your very loss.

That is how much I think of you,

so much, because my love is true.

But remember I have risen,

and from my throne, I will alleviate your prison.

So continue your prayers to me up above,

for I give you my help, but most of all, my love.

JESUS

(Inspired by a woman who was battered)

ONWARD

It's time for you to smile,

time, because my friend, it has been awhile.

Don't let life get you down;

you're too special to keep that frown.

There are people who do care,

so accept the love and joy they wish to share.

You had your time to cry,

now it's your time to fly.

Pick yourself up, I believe in you,

don't hesitate, take part in the happiness that is your due.

Today's a new day get up and fight,

show the world your inner might.

With God and friends at your side,

it is time for you to turn the tide.

MADE IN THE IMAGE OF GOD

Long before the world began,

God said now we will create man.

Let us make him in our image,

and populate the world with a holy lineage.

Then he made them male and female,

using his likeness for the scale.

He formed the man from the clay in the ground,

breathed life in his nostrils and a soul was found.

He cast a sleep on him and took out a rib,

and from that bone sculpted a woman to join the Eden crib.

Given beauty, joy, and peace in the garden,

all was well till they needed a pardon.

Warned not to eat the apple was God's command,

but they ate it anyway and were quickly banned.

Beauty and peace were lost that day,

and all the ugliness of sin was here to stay.

Sloth, anger, gluttony, and lust,

were among the sins to break God's trust.

Beautiful and white as snow was their soul,

it now turned repulsive and dark as coal.

From that day sin began,

destroying what God had in his plan.

With each sin mankind engages in,

he tarnishes his soul from within.

Bright and beautiful on the day of birth,

it soon dims losing its worth.

Days, weeks, and years, pass by,

as man lives while sentencing his soul to die.

Selfishness, bigotry, and many a vice,

the individual no longer is the image of God, and pays the price.

Loneliness, depression, worry, anger, and more,

as every evil and paranoid emotion eat at his core.

He lives in an endless cycle not listening to the Lord,

producing sins outside himself, while inside, there is discord.

His body grows tense,

from the angered epithets he will dispense.

Or falls bent,

by the pangs he will lament.

At times there is a profuse sweat,

from each and every fret.

The body will tremble and shake,

from all the alcohol, drugs, and false cures it will take.

The once beautiful soul of a baby first born,

will become a mixture of emotions that will culminate with forlorn.

God looks down from the heavens and sees mankind in need,

the beautiful image he created, has been warped by the evil deed.

Billions of souls on the earth no longer look like God,

running around in helplessness, until the Almighty gives the nod;

I made them in my image the day creation began,

now I'll wipe out sin and restore my likeness back to man.

So on that day a new creation came,

and salvation was its very name.

To return mankind as angelic as before,

he sent his only son to earth on a mission to restore.

So the passion of Christ did begin,

to erase each and every sin.

And when he died on the cross,

it was more than enough to cover the loss.

On that day all of the blood that flowed,

washed away the sin where the soul makes its abode.

Thus the darkness was lifted and the ugliness made to disappear,

and the souls returned to their brilliance, when God held up the eternal mirror.

BEGIN AGAIN

Don't you worry or stress,

life is filled with troubles and mess.

Take things day by day,

rely on family, friends, and God for the way.

Never let things get you down,

realize life's true priorities, and reverse that frown.

Troubles come and go,

but the love from people that care will always grow.

So remember when you feel blue,

weigh life's true worth, and start anew!

I AM THE RESSURECTION AND THE LIFE

Lord, my world is crushing in on me,

I am alone, depressed, the pain hurts, can't you see?

My troubles give me no rest,

I don't know where to turn, I am helpless at best.

Filled with dread, worry, and fear,

the pain is so deep, I cannot cry another tear.

Never lose faith in me,

do you think after all I have done, I would abandon thee?

You may not know what path to take,

but do not think I left you, my love is not fake.

When in the dark one knows not where to go,

so they remain helpless, confined, a prisoner to only the darkness they know.

But there is a story I want you to keep in mind,

then in this darkness, your way out you'll find.

Many years ago a man named Lazarus was very sick,

his family summoned the Lord to heal him, and to come quick.

But Jesus stayed put and did not take flight,

rather, he waited until the time was right.

When he finally arrived Lazarus had already died,

he was so moved, he even cried.

But he told the man's sister her brother would rise,

that he who believes in me, never ever dies.

As they made their way to where the body was,

the air was filled with a curious buzz,

Many wondered why Lazarus had to die,

couldn't this Jesus have done something to save this guy?

When Jesus saw the sister was still in grief,

he told her that she lacked belief.

Though Lazarus had been dead four days and all were filled with gloom,

he told them to remove the stone that was blocking the tomb.

At the entrance of the cave where Lazarus was laid,

he raised his eyes to heaven and quietly prayed.

Then in a loud voice he said, *"Lazarus, come out!"*

and shortly after, the dead man walked about.

Still tied hand and foot in burial bands,

"Untie him, let him go," was the second of his commands.

Now listen, I don't just call Lazarus to come out,

I call each of you by name, with a loving shout.

I call you from sickness, loneliness, rising bills,

addictions, broken hearts, alcohol, and pills.

I call you from despair, frustration, and pain,

injustice, hunger, handicaps, my call will never wane.

I call you from selfishness, greed, and power,

lust, hatred, jealousy, I call you every hour.

I call you from all that keeps you bound,

I call you for a new life to be found.

So when the darkness has surrounded you,

listen for your name, so my voice can come through.

Like Lazarus rise from the dead of your past and start anew,

untie those deadly bands that bind like glue.

Search for me when you see no light,

I am on the outside, guiding you through your night.

So from the death that is all about,

I am calling your name, saying, "Come out!"

FAITH

Loneliness and depression came to me,

from the troubles that would not let me be.

I have been the victim of their fate,

crying myself to sleep when it would get late.

Looking for help I prayed to the Lord,

but silence is the reply that he chose to afford.

I made up my mind that if he wasn't going to speak,

that I would not give up, but continue to seek.

For I didn't trust my eyes or how I felt,

but in his words, and his promise of salvation if I knelt.

So on my knees I prayed and cried,

weekly, monthly, yearly, my answers still denied.

Often I felt at the end of my rope,

still the prayers gave me a glimmer of hope.

Not knowing how I would make it another day,

it was that glimmer that began to show me the way.

I followed this minute ray of light,

amidst all the darkness, it began to shine bright.

I still struggled long and hard,

but kept clinging to that hope, to carry me the extra yard.

When once I felt so low,

I now began to see a possibility grow.

As I look back on how far I came,

and how I made it, its Jesus that gets the acclaim.

When I struggled with no end to my miseries in sight,

I recalled his words to keep up the fight.

When my pain was too much to bear,

I knew that on my cross, he still did care.

Many nights I waited for him to rescue me from all the pain,

and wondered why his heavenly hand would continue to refrain.

But it wasn't until my last fall,

when it finally came to me that he did give me his all.

From his birth to the cross when he breathed his last,

he showed me how to live the present, trust the future, and forget the past.

His whole life is the medicine for every ill,

giving us the nourishment to strengthen our will.

He grants us wisdom to choose what is best,

and is the inspiration when we cannot rest.

All this time I was looking for a fast easy way out,

but now I know, this is not what following Christ is all about.

Following his example and the words that he gave,

is what he left us on how he would save.

So I will fight the good fight and follow his lead,

with faith no bigger than a mustard seed.

Some say my thinking goes out on a limb,

but I remain confident, because I have faith in him.

THE GREAT GIFT

You had ill health and were often in bed,

but I nursed your soul, and it was never dead.

Your family had left you and there was no one around,

but all alone, your friendship I found.

When you labored long and hard for barely a cent,

it was heavenly riches that I quickly lent.

You often complained, thinking your prayers were ignored,

but it was then that your petitions had truly soared.

When you felt full of despair,

it was I nearby who was always there.

When you were hurt and your heart was breaking,

you didn't realize that it was true character in the making.

As you can see, you thought you had always gone it alone,

but I watched with esteem, on how much you had grown.

In this life you felt you were at the end of the line,

but the blessings handed out, that started there, were mine.

What I gave you, you could not see,

but look closely, what I gave to you, is me.

JESUS

ONE QUESTION FROM GOD

Before time began I created you with a thought,

because my love for you had me uncontrollably caught.

Thus it was my plan that we would be together forever,

but I want you to make your own choice, do you want me too, or never?

So when I formed you I gave you a free will,

to choose me, or look elsewhere to get your fill.

But my love for you is so great,

I sent many blessings to give you a sample of a heavenly fate.

The gifts I send come in different shapes and sizes,

and if you focus on what you have been given, you'll see many surprises.

Among some of the treasures that I did bestow,

wisdom, health, life, family, friends, besides the future ones that I will show.

I guided your life to be in a better place,

and when you didn't listen and fell, I quickly gave chase.

I would pick you up from how far you sank,

purify your soul and return its rank.

When you forget me and go on your way,

I wait for your return, hoping you would come back to stay.

Often you spend no time with me until you are in a jam,

then you seek me out, saying, Lord, here I am.

When things don't go your way, you blame me and get mad,

even refusing to talk to me, like I have done something bad.

You forget me more then I care to mention,

even when the world makes you ill and I try a spiritual intervention.

Once in a while you'll speak to me when you are alone,

but in public your affection for me is never shown.

When you are with friends,

your embarrassment for me never ends.

You scoff at my ways and assume they are wrong,

but they are to test your will and make you strong.

I always wanted you to be near,

but when you go on your own, I still hold you dear.

I promised you eternal life and all the riches it supplies,

but you preferred the devil's garbage, that's not even fit for the flies.

So I did something never before seen,

to show you just how much you do mean.

As a person gives someone they love a picture of a heart,

I am giving you an image of mine I hope will never depart.

Close your eyes and look at my visual card,

you will see me on the cross, crucified by the Roman guard.

Nails are pounded in my hands and feet,

my body whipped, broken, and violently beat.

My face gaunt and pale,

mouth agape, as my lungs fail.

My eyes half glazed and dim,

death has risen to the brim.

Patches in my beard are bloody and bare,

where they tugged, pulled, and ripped out the hair.

Teeth chipped and cracked from their blows,

bruised, contusions, and lumps, they have broken my nose.

Lips are puffy, eyes swollen shut,

while blood gushes from my head, where the thorns have deeply cut.

My features covered in their spittle,

compassion was not shown to me, not even a little.

Enticing you to be with me, this gesture will be my last try,

there is nothing more that I can do, then to this way; die.

So look at me now and what my heart is made of,

and I ask you one question, am I so hard for you to love?

THE CALL OF THE LORD

Do not weep when someone dies,

for that is when their soul flies.

Remember death has no power,

for only the Lord can call our hour.

When we come to the end of our life,

the Lord smiles, saying, now ends your strife.

Long and hard you have labored in this land,

now it's time to receive your reward for following my command.

Part one of your life is done,

and part two has just begun.

For I will transform your life into a beautiful spirit,

with my call, as soon as you hear it.

You who have been heavily burdened in this earthly quest,

are now to receive an eternal rest.

No more tears, no more fears,

just peace and happiness with your heavenly peers.

So it is the sweet soothing voice of the Lord that sets us free,

when he whispers to us, come, and follow me.

TGIF

Thank God it's Friday,

is what the worker will say.

For as soon as the job is done,

they go out for a weekend of fun.

But true thanks to the Lord,

Requires more from us to afford.

It should start when we first arise,

till at night, when we close our eyes.

For it was before time began,

when God wrote our name into the divine plan.

Since then his blessings did flow,

choosing us for them to bestow.

Taking care of our spiritual wealth,

not to mention our earthly health.

Family, friends, and good Samaritans sent to our door,

when we were in need and didn't even implore.

Given our senses,

not to mention the graces he dispenses.

Plus wisdom to pray,

and a heart to share every day.

Our mistakes and sins forgiven so we can start anew,

by caring friends, family, and a personal Savior too.

Blessings continue from morning to night,

from our birth, to our final light.

And for all of this people say,

thank God, it's Friday.

So let us render our thanks not just for a weekend mood,

for there is so much more we need to show our gratitude.

And finally let us never forget for our sins he did pay,

and for this we exclaim, thank God, for that Good Friday.

TURN THE OTHER CHEEK

My disciple, turn the other cheek,

this is the rule that I want you to seek.

I am not referring to when you are struck with a blow,

but in everything that you do, for you reap what you sow.

Every difficulty in life presents to you a door,

one is the devil's, and one is mine, but be careful how you explore.

Those who enter his, never come out the same,

if they even come out at all, is what the devil will exclaim.

His way looks easy and to be a quick fix,

but choose it once, and for life, you will be taking your licks.

Choose mine, and your efforts will appear tenfold,

having to use your will, instead of the short cuts the devil has sold.

But you will be like gold tested in fire, coming out more pure than before,

and this is the reward you receive, in choosing my door.

So be wary when the devil presents to you an easy way to take,

because in truth, it is not done for you, but for his own sake.

He had made the same choice when given his test,

and now full of suffering and hatred, your downfall is his quest.

So when a temptation or cross comes to you,

turn to me, to help make it through:

When you bear the pangs of hunger and thirst,

divert from this craving, and feed thy soul till it burst.

If you feel lazy and wish to thwart a good deed,

look at how I carried the cross, then follow my lead.

Should a sensuous image spark in you a lustful notion,

cast thy glance at my beaten flesh, and increase your devotion.

If you are abandoned and feeling lonely,

shift your eyes from this solitude, and say, God only.

When a love has broken your heart,

remember mine pierced with a lance, and do not depart.

When someone close to you dies,

steer away from the sadness of death, to my promise, that all shall arise.

When depression strikes you to the ground,

change your direction upward, to the salvation you have found.

Follow this rule when the inevitable cross comes your way,

and I will be there waiting, to help you carry it another day.

And when your life is finally done,

your sins and deeds will be tallied to the very last one.

And should your life be found wanting and your eternity looks bleak,

fear not faithful disciple, for I too, will turn the other cheek.

THE LAST JUDGMENT

The day I closed my eyes and died,

I was presented before the judge to be tried.

I approached the gate and stood very still,

except for my knees knocking as I felt a chill.

St. Peter stood before me and held a book in his hand,

saying, "we shall see if you sink in the abyss, or enter the Promised Land.

In these pages is your life both good and bad,

and you will be judged by what is written in this pad."

Then my guardian angel stood at my right,

the devil on the left was a terrible sight.

"Your angel will help plead your case," St. Peter said,

"but the devil will accuse you, fighting till you are eternally dead."

Then he read out of the book,

and from my head to my toes, my whole body shook.

He read off the prayers that I recited,

as well as the good deeds that I had ignited.

The help that I gave to those in need,

and the remorse I had shown, for breaking God's creed.

The devil laughed and said the book was right,

but wanted to offer some additional light.

He said, while I prayed mostly every day,

they were short, said fast, and with a mind that would stray.

The deeds I did were far and few,

as I overlooked more opportunities then I knew.

As for the help that I had gave,

it was but a small percent on how I should behave.

And the remorse shown when I would sin,

he said it was as much from my getting caught, as from within.

He said every bad word, thought, and deed,

far outweighed the one, "I am sorry," and that St. Peter should take heed.

Then my angel spoke,

"what the devil says is no joke.

While it's true this soul's goods are outweighed,

 in the end, he was on his knees and prayed."

Then the devil jumped back in,

reciting a list of each and every sin.

Foul language, lust, gossip, lies,

anger, sloth, cheating, and not breaking with evil ties.

Selfishness, greed, jealousy, and more,

the devil spoke for over an hour, as he kept score.

Then he held up a cross of Jesus crucified,

gave it to St. Peter and replied.

"Are you going to let him get away with this?
for all of his sins, he deserves no eternal bliss."

With a strong grip the devil started to take me away,
and snarled quietly, "I knew you would pay."
I pleaded with St. Peter for one more chance,
but he shook his head and sadly turned his glance.
He said, your time for retribution is already done,
that is what your work on earth is for my son.
The devil sank his claws deep into my arm,
the pain was like five sharp needles and he smiled at
the harm.
My flesh started to burn from the touch,
and I tried to pull away from his clutch.
When he leaned in my ear and spoke,
I thought the temperature from his breath would make
me choke.
"The first thing I will do is throw you into a pit of fire,
then toss in piles and piles of the nastiest mire.
You will know how much your sins stink,
when in this filth you begin to sink.
Past rotting souls will swim to you and hold you down,
as they try to stay afloat and not endlessly drown.
After doing this for several years,
I will think up for you new and worse fears."

I yelled and struggled for him to let me go,

and begged St. Peter, true repentance I would show.

Then the devil's grip loosened and he became weak,

I turned and saw Jesus standing next to my cheek.

"Lord, it's true, I threw my whole life away,

but you can save me, you have the final say.

Please, I beg you have mercy on me,

have mercy on a soul who didn't try to see."

Then he wiped away my tear,

and looked in my eyes if I was sincere.

When I saw his hand, and in it the bloody hole,

I exclaimed, "it is true! You have done this for my soul!"

He nodded, then showed me his feet and side,

to win your love, everything I have tried.

I saw spit on his face,

lacerations all over the place.

Thorns in his head,

and though he was silent, it was, "I love you," that he said.

Seeing the great love that he applied,

I knew that I was unworthy to be by his side.

Sobbing; "I deserve the pains of hell,"

and with that, on my knees I fell.

"No matter what punishment is my due,

I am so sorry, for what I have done to you!"

I then felt my arm snatched,

and knew the time for my punishment was to be hatched.

When I got to my feet,

the devil already made a hasty retreat.

Around my arm was the wounded hand,

for it was Jesus who had helped me to stand.

I gave him a befuddled look,

and he pointed back to St. Peter's book.

On the pages where my sins were listed,

blood covered the words, and he smiled and said, "*I insisted.*"

TRUE HAPPINESS

For a few minutes of a sinful pleasure,

you have traded your heavenly treasure.

Now that you have hit your high,

tell me, was it worth it for your soul to die?

All the joy lasted for a brief time,

and lost is an eternal sublime.

Don't you realize that whenever the devil will speak,

you stand to lose what you truly seek?

It isn't drugs, loose sex, or alcohol,

nor power, vengeance, or money at all.

For these seemingly bring a certain relief and joy,

but these are not real, but merely a ploy.

The happiness isn't that strong,

and the effects of these do not last very long.

They often come with a lot of regret and pain,

and one never indulges in them with a gain.

But the happiness and peace that is truly complete,

lies nowhere else, but at the Lord's feet.

It doesn't fill up a beastly passion,

but overflows the soul in a divinely fashion.

This love that the Lord gives no one can explain,

and no earthly pleasure will ever attain.

Do not trade what will corrode,

for all the Lord gives in his heavenly abode.

THE WAY TO HEAVEN

Entering past the heavenly gate,

is the unclaimed prize of the reprobate.

For they lived all their life as they had wanted,

now in their eternity they will remain forever haunted.

While you denied your ways with self-control,

this is the way of life that I did extol.

All the work on earth by your hand,

has brought you to the Promised Land.

It was the coins you gave to the poor,

that have placed you at the heavenly door.

The forgiveness you offered to those who offended,

causing me to overlook your sins, and our friendship was mended.

When you gave a shoulder to a crying soul in need,

it placed you from the back of the Christian line, and to the lead.

Taking time to guide one who was lost,

saved you from a terrible cost.

And when you fell from my grace,

you immediately dropped on your knees and quickly saved face.

What brought you to this heavenly bliss,

was not great works or many noble tasks, no, not any of this.

But following my way the best you can,

and doing what I taught, as the plan.

The little simple method of taking up your cross and following me,

has rewarded you with heavenly joy, for all eternity.

THE LIGHT OF CHRIST

Let your light shine before man,

show them my image as much as you can.

Though everyone is created the same,

when you follow me, you represent my name.

So hold yourself to a standard much higher,

avoid the least of sins, giving an example to admire.

As my follower be eager to help those in need,

like a Samaritan planting the Christian seed.

No deed is too small,

so in everything you do, give it your all.

Perform all of your actions with lots of love,

than everyone will know you belong to the one above.

Preach faith, hope, and charity,

so all who see you, will see me.

There will be many times when this lifestyle will be rough,

and a lesser man will leave in a huff.

But stay my course even when you had enough,

for with me, my saints and martyrs were supernaturally tough.

Don't let mankind or life get you down,

be full of enthusiasm, strong of will, and you will wear the heavenly crown.

Let not the slightest transgression escape from your lip,

lest you sin further and continue to slip.

For the child of God may live on earth,

but their mind is focused on a greater worth.

They know that my blessings and love are a treasure,

a priceless value one can never measure.

Thus illuminate my life in this world of darkness and despair,

so all may see it like a spiritual flare.

Shine the light brightly on me and the example that I give,

so others will follow, and know how to live.

HELL

Deep in the caverns of hell,

are the souls who fell.

They scream and wail,

as the flames burn their flesh in the eternal jail.

The heat suffocates as they gasp for air,

but this is just the beginning for those in the devil's lair.

Days, years, centuries, pass by,

as every second they continue to die.

Their mouths will become parched from their incessant screams,

of the nightmares they live, that once were their dreams.

Flames flicker in the pitch black caves,

flashing glimpses of hideous images of the devil's tormented slaves.

All the money, sex, hatred, and power, that made them kings on earth,

do nothing for them now, in the low hellish berth.

Smoke fills their lungs and burns their eyes,

while their ears ring from the echo of distant bemoaning cries.

In their nostrils is the smell of rotting flesh,

and this is the air they breathe to refresh.

At times the caverns become deathly frigid,

as decades pass and their limbs remain rigid.

Vapors emit as the cold fills their lungs,

their teeth chattering out curses with frozen tongues.

Their bodies remain twisted and contorted,

their faces grim and grossly distorted.

All the pain, anger, and regret,

have mangled their limbs because of a sinful debt.

They will suffer all alone,

from those nearby, no compassion will be shown.

The devil will mock them for their choice,

when on earth, they dismissed God, in lieu of the evil voice.

All of the fun and enticements the world gave,

is but a chain in the devil's cave.

A chain they can never break,

because not choosing God, was the irreversible mistake.

In the darkness all around,

they will hear a most disturbing sound.

It will be the inner voice of their soul,

that will take the hardest toll.

For the greatest torment that they will sigh,

is the loss of a loving savior, who for these very sins did die.

More love than all the mothers combined have for a child,

Is no longer theirs, having refused to be reconciled.

Instead they will suffer by the devil and his imps,

losing the loving embrace of the Lord, and a heavenly glimpse.

They will see all the mercy, grace, and commandments, God gave for them to choose,

and the inspirations, callings, and knowledge of Christ's death, so heaven they wouldn't lose.

And of their denial and ignoring all his loving tries,

for a mere gratification, from the father of lies.

The cross that they so often ran from on earth,

they now realize was the road to their heavenly birth.

This is their lot for all eternity,

knowing this loving Jesus, they will never see.

THE MIRACLE MAN
(An eye witness testimony)

In Nazareth there is a man that everyone is talking about,
some love him, some hate him, so I had to find out.
I had followed him for more than a year,
and know well his story, for I was very near.
In the crowds I had heard him preach,
and it is all about love that he would teach.
The compassion in his voice strikes your heart,
while the wisdom in his words sets him far apart.
He speaks with authority one cannot deny,
and only the foolish accuse him of any lie.

He has done many things that have baffled the mind,
and each and every one of them is nothing but kind.
He healed a man with a withered hand,
has made a lame fellow get up and stand.
He cured a leper with a touch,
and for some healings, he didn't even do that much!
For a centurion's distant servant he merely said a word,
and the man was healed through this Christ, whose voice he never heard.
Once a woman with a hemorrhage touched his cloak,
and was instantly healed, though he never spoke.

He has changed water into wine,

sent demons into a group of swine.

He walked on water,

and saved a woman about to be stoned, from a horrible slaughter.

Fed five thousand with fives loaves and two fish,

and all that was required, was that he bless the dish.

He calmed a storm on the sea,

and cast out demons to set the afflicted free.

When I thought I had seen it all,

he did something that made even these look small.

An official told him his daughter was dead,

so he went to his house, and she arose from the bed.

To another he did the same,

raising a man from a tomb, just by calling his name.

Then after conquering death,

this man of wonders once again took my breath.

It was Friday when I heard they took him to trial,

I wasn't worried, I knew he would be out in a short while.

Later news circulated that he was sentenced to die,

but I knew better, this man had powers with the blink of an eye.

When I learned he was on his way to Calvary,

I had to go and find out what new miracle there would be.

As I arrived I saw an angry mob,

and beheld a sight that caused me to sob.

There was a man beaten beyond compare,

his face and body distorted, blood was everywhere.

Upon his shoulder a beam so heavy it forced him to the ground,

as I gazed even harder, it was the man of miracles that I had found!

I waited for him to say a word or raise his hand,

wondering how much more of this he would stand.

For he well had the power,

to change this darkest hour.

But he did nothing to stop the brutality,

and waived his power to be free.

Next, the hands that healed so many were firmly nailed,

and the feet that walked on water, were equally impaled.

The voice that spoke and raised the dead,

was silent, as he dropped his head.

As I watched how he had died,

it came to me why escape he hadn't tried.

For all of the love and forgiveness that he had preached,

it was the cross that he knew more souls would be reached.

Even the centurion who crucified him on that notorious lot,

was converted shortly after, on the very spot.

Many more conversions soon followed,

as he took a tragic event and had made it hallowed.

So even death has not stopped his ways,

for he was to perform one of his greatest miracles, in just three days!

THE REPENTANT SINNER

Lord, I ignored all that you taught,

for the drugs, sex, and alcohol, that I had sought.

I went about my life doing things my way,

having too much fun to spend time to pray.

At first this lifestyle seemed so great,

but I was fooled, and had taken the devil's bait.

In the beginning he turned me from you,

oh, not a lot, just an inch or two.

Slowly the inch grew to a foot, and then a yard,

till I traveled far away, and my heart grew hard.

Often I was promiscuous, drunk, and high,

it wasn't until years later, when I found out the lie.

Addictions, desperation, loneliness and despair,

became my new friends, till I realized they didn't care.

The peace and happiness that I once held sublime,

became a thing of my past, lost in time.

The sins grew and attacked my heart and mind,

leaving suffering and pain all that was left to find.

Through so many years of continued crying,

I decided once more to adopt your way, and began trying.

Hoping it was not too late,

and that you would save me from a deadly fate.

The first act was to call your name,

and then on my knees, the prayers came.

Child, sin has cast its shadow over you,
painting a silhouette of an unrecognizable hue.
A face of hurt and sadness,
born from loneliness, despair, and restless madness.
This is not the countenance of those who belong to me,
but the expressions of the ones who are in sinful captivity.
Now you turned from your life of dissipation,
and the angels sang out in heavenly elation.
So many tears fell about,
since that day from my heart, when you ran out.
Now I will make your soul white as snow,
purifying it from the many graces that will flow.
The ills that have made you sick,
I will erase, and make you angelic.

Suddenly I saw Christ on the cross struggling for breath,

enduring a most excruciating and undeserved death.

Each of his limbs were bound with a nail,

his life ebbing away, as his face grew pale.

He winced in agony and grimaced with every movement,

but any attempts to shift his body, offered no improvement.

Blood gushed from his wounds like a waterfall of red,

and I knew in just seconds he would soon be dead.

I approached and watched as he was dying,

when my health returned, I realized this was the cure he was applying.

My gaze arose until it met his glance,

I wanted to thank him for giving me one more chance.

But I could not speak,

nor he, who was too weak.

His arms moved forward to give me a hug,

but the nails kept his limbs painfully snug.

Shortly after, he bowed his head and died,

and for my sins, I had truly cried.

Time had passed and I changed my life,

the image of my Lord, had cut me like a knife.

It was a spiritual wound that never healed,

causing my debauchery to finally yield.

I prayed more,

and now, the least of my sins, I do abhor.

Peace and happiness came to me,

and gone was the misery.

I lived this way for many years,

no longer sorrow, but joy, were my new tears.

When my time had finally come and on my judgement I did rise, a misty haze dissipated, and heaven was before my eyes.

As the clouds disappeared,

a distant figure neared.

I raised my gaze to his face,

and beheld the Lord, standing in his place.

He looked at me for a little while,

and then gave the most welcoming smile.

His arms reached forward no longer bound,

as we hugged, he whispered, *"Now, you are found."*

LORD, LET ME WALK ON WATER

You guide me from my will and the dangers it brings,
and should I fall into the abyss of my weaknesses,
you reach out your hand and pull me up to safety.

With you nothing holds me down. I transcend the impossible.

Call unto me oh Lord, and I will walk on water for Thee.

www.ingramcontent.com/pod-product-compliance
Lightning Source LLC
LaVergne TN
LVHW021546080426
835509LV00019B/2863